ARCTIC FOX

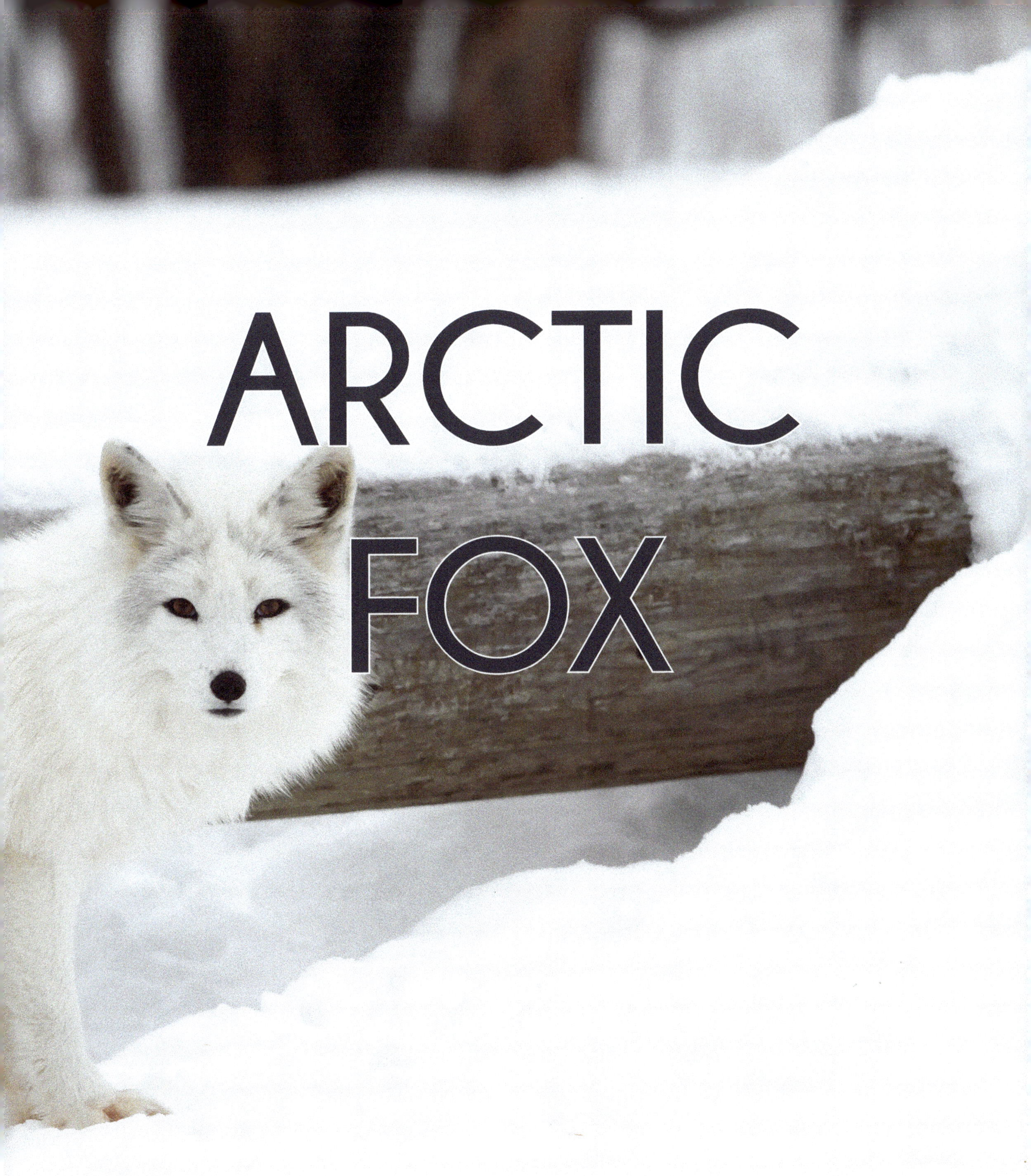

Dylanna Press

ISBN: 978-1647900182 (pb); 978-1647904494 (hc)
Publisher: Dylanna Publishing, Inc.
First Edition: 2020
10 9 8 7 6 5 4 3 2 1

For information about special discounts for bulk purchases, please contact:

orders@dylannapublishing.com
Dylanna Publishing, Inc.
www.dylannapublishing.com

Contents

Meet the Arctic Fox

CRUNCH! Picture yourself trudging through knee-deep snow in temperatures so cold your breath freezes the moment it leaves your lips. The wind howls across an endless white landscape where winter lasts nine months and the sun disappears for weeks at a time. Suddenly, a flash of white fur bursts from beneath the snow. A small, fluffy creature with bright eyes and a bushy tail vanishes before you can blink. Welcome to the world of the Arctic fox!

These remarkable little hunters thrive in some of the harshest places on Earth. You'll find them roaming the frozen tundra of Alaska, Canada, Russia, Scandinavia, Greenland, and Iceland. In these regions, winter temperatures can plunge to –58°F (–50°C), and blizzards can bury the land under deep snow.

Their scientific name is *Vulpes lagopus*. It means "hare-footed fox," a nod to the thick fur covering their paws like built-in snow boots. Arctic foxes belong to the Canidae family, which makes them relatives of dogs, wolves, and other foxes.

Arctic Fox vs **Red Fox**

Arctic foxes live in the frozen tundra and polar regions of the Northern Hemisphere.

Arctic foxes are small, compact foxes with short ears and short noses that help conserve heat.

Arctic foxes change fur color with the seasons—white in winter and brown or gray in summer.

Arctic foxes are adapted for life in harsh Arctic environments, even during long, dark winters.

Red foxes live in forests, grasslands, deserts, and even cities around the world.

Red foxes are larger and slimmer, with longer ears and noses that help release heat.

Red foxes keep their reddish-brown fur year-round for camouflage in many habitats.

Red foxes are highly adaptable animals that thrive near humans and in changing environments.

What makes them so incredible? Arctic foxes can survive temperatures that would freeze most animals solid. Their thick fur changes color with the seasons. In winter, it turns snow-white for perfect camouflage. In summer, it becomes brown or gray to blend in with rocks and plants. Arctic foxes have the warmest fur of any mammal on Earth, even warmer than polar bears.

For thousands of years, these tough little survivors have inspired Arctic peoples. Today, climate change is making their frozen world smaller and more unpredictable. Scientists are working to understand how Arctic foxes are adapting and how protecting their habitat can help ensure these amazing animals continue to thrive in the years ahead.

Built for the Frozen North

Arctic foxes are small but mighty, perfectly designed for life in extreme cold.

One of the smallest members of the Canidae family, Arctic foxes weigh just 6 to 15 pounds (2.7 to 6.8 kilograms) and measure 18 to 26 inches long (46 to 66 centimeters), not counting their bushy tails. That's about the size of a house cat. Males are slightly larger than females, but both are compact and low to the ground.

Everything about their body helps them conserve precious heat. Their legs are short and sturdy. Their ears are small and rounded, unlike the tall, pointy ears of a red fox, which means less surface area for heat to escape. Their muzzle is short and their face is almost flat, reducing exposed skin.

And then there's that magnificent tail. An Arctic fox's tail can be up to 13 inches long (33 centimeters), nearly as long as its body. This fluffy wonder serves multiple purposes. It helps with balance when running and jumping, but more importantly, it works like a built-in blanket. When an Arctic fox curls up to sleep, it wraps that big bushy tail around its face and paws, creating a cozy pocket of warmth against the howling wind.

DID YOU KNOW?

Arctic foxes are the only members of the dog family with fur-covered foot pads. This furry footwear helps them walk on ice without slipping—and without freezing their toes off!

Their paws are completely covered in thick fur, even on the bottoms. This gives them grip on slippery ice and protects their feet from frostbite. It's like wearing fuzzy snow boots everywhere you go.

Where Do Arctic Foxes Live?

Arctic foxes make their home in the frozen lands that circle the top of the world. Their territory stretches across the Arctic regions of North America, Europe, and Asia, anywhere the ground stays frozen and winters are long and severe.

You'll find them padding across the snowy landscapes of Alaska, northern Canada, Greenland, Iceland, Norway, Sweden, Finland, and Russia. Arctic foxes are the only land mammal native to Iceland, having walked there across frozen sea ice thousands of years ago.

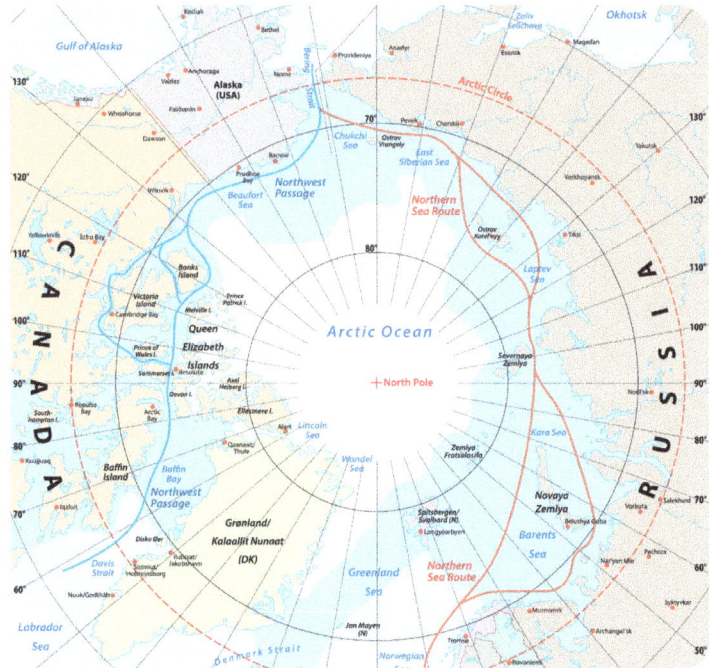

Arctic foxes live on land throughout the Arctic tundra regions shown around the North Pole, including Alaska, northern Canada, Greenland, Scandinavia, Iceland, and Russia.

These tough little foxes live in the tundra, a treeless, frozen plain where temperatures regularly drop below –22°F (–30°C) and can plunge to a bone-chilling –58°F (–50°C). In winter, the Arctic becomes a world of endless white, with snow covering nearly everything and the sun barely rising above the horizon for months at a time.

Some Arctic foxes are true nomads, wandering hundreds of miles across sea ice in search of food. Others stay closer to home, living in the same territory year after year. Coastal foxes may even follow polar bears onto the sea ice, hoping to scavenge leftovers from seal hunts.

During the brief Arctic summer, the tundra transforms. Snow melts to reveal wildflowers, grasses, and shrubs. The sun shines around the clock, creating 24 hours of daylight. Arctic foxes shed their white coats and turn brown or gray to blend in with this new landscape.

Fun Fact: Arctic foxes can travel more than 600 miles (1,000 kilometers) across sea ice in search of food.

Fun Fact: An arctic fox's winter coat has about 20,000 hairs per square centimeter—that's more hairs in a space the size of your pinky fingernail than you have on your entire head!

Super Survivors: Arctic Fox Adaptations

Arctic foxes have incredible features that help them survive where most animals would freeze solid.

The World's Warmest Coat

Arctic fox fur is the warmest of any mammal, even warmer than polar bear fur. Their coat has two layers: a dense, fluffy undercoat that traps air close to the skin and longer guard hairs on top that shed snow and ice. This insulation is so effective that Arctic foxes do not start shivering until temperatures drop below –94°F (–70°C).

Color-Changing Fur

Their coat changes with the seasons. In winter, most Arctic foxes turn pure white to blend in with the snow. In summer, they shed that white fur and grow brown or gray coats to match the tundra's rocks and plants. Some foxes, called blue morphs, stay bluish-gray all year.

Furry Feet

Thick fur covers their paw pads, giving them traction on slippery ice and protecting their feet from frozen ground. It is like wearing built-in snow boots.

Heat-Saving Shape

Short legs, small rounded ears, and a compact body help reduce heat loss. Less exposed surface area means more warmth stays inside.

Super Hearing

Arctic foxes can hear prey moving beneath the snow from several feet away. They tilt their head, pinpoint the sound, and leap straight down to catch their meal.

Fat Reserves

Before winter, Arctic foxes eat as much as possible and can gain up to 50 percent more body weight. This extra fat provides insulation and energy when food becomes scarce.

What Do Arctic Foxes Eat?

Arctic foxes are omnivores, which means they will eat almost anything they can find. In the harsh Arctic, being a picky eater is not an option.

Their favorite food is lemmings, small rodents that live in tunnels beneath the snow. When lemming populations are high, Arctic foxes feast. A single fox might eat a dozen lemmings in one day. However, lemming populations rise and fall dramatically, so Arctic foxes must be flexible hunters.

These clever predators also catch voles, squirrels, birds, and bird eggs. Near the coast, they snatch fish from shallow waters or dig up shellfish along the beach. They may even raid seabird nesting colonies to eat eggs and chicks.

When hunting is poor, Arctic foxes become scavengers. They often follow polar bears across the sea ice, waiting for leftovers from seal kills. Polar bears usually eat only the fat-rich blubber, leaving plenty of meat behind for hungry foxes. In desperate times, Arctic foxes will also eat berries, seaweed, and even the droppings of other animals.

DID YOU KNOW?

Arctic foxes have been seen following polar bears for days, patiently waiting at a safe distance for the bear to make a kill. One scientist watched a fox trail a polar bear for over 90 miles across the sea ice—that's some serious dedication to a free meal!

One of their most important survival strategies is food caching. During summer and fall, when food is plentiful, Arctic foxes bury extra meals in the frozen ground. This natural deep freezer allows them to store birds, eggs, and lemmings and dig them up later when winter makes hunting difficult.

Fun Fact: Arctic foxes can store hundreds of food items underground to survive the long winter months.

Fun Fact: Scientists have found that Arctic foxes hunt more accurately when they pounce toward the northeast.

The Hunt

Arctic foxes are skilled predators with incredible senses that make them deadly hunters, even in a world buried under snow.

Their hunting technique is one of nature's most spectacular shows. An Arctic fox trots across the snowy tundra with its head tilted and ears swiveling like satellite dishes. It listens for the tiny sounds of lemmings scurrying through tunnels beneath the snow. When it pinpoints its target, the fox freezes. It stands perfectly still, using its sensitive ears to locate the exact position of its prey.

Then comes the pounce. The fox leaps high into the air with its front legs extended and dives nose-first into the snow. It punches through the crust with its sharp snout and snatches the surprised lemming before it can escape. Scientists call this technique "mousing," and Arctic foxes have perfected it into an art form.

This hunting style requires incredible precision. The fox must determine where its prey is hiding using sound alone, then launch itself at exactly the right angle to break through the snow and reach the tunnel below. It is like catching something you cannot see.

MYTH VS FACT

Arctic foxes hunt by sight alone.

MYTH

Arctic foxes rely heavily on their hearing and can detect prey moving beneath thick layers of snow.

FACT

Arctic foxes also hunt above ground. They chase birds, stalk nesting geese, and ambush ptarmigan hiding in low vegetation. Near water, they wade into shallow streams to catch fish or patrol beaches for washed-up marine life.

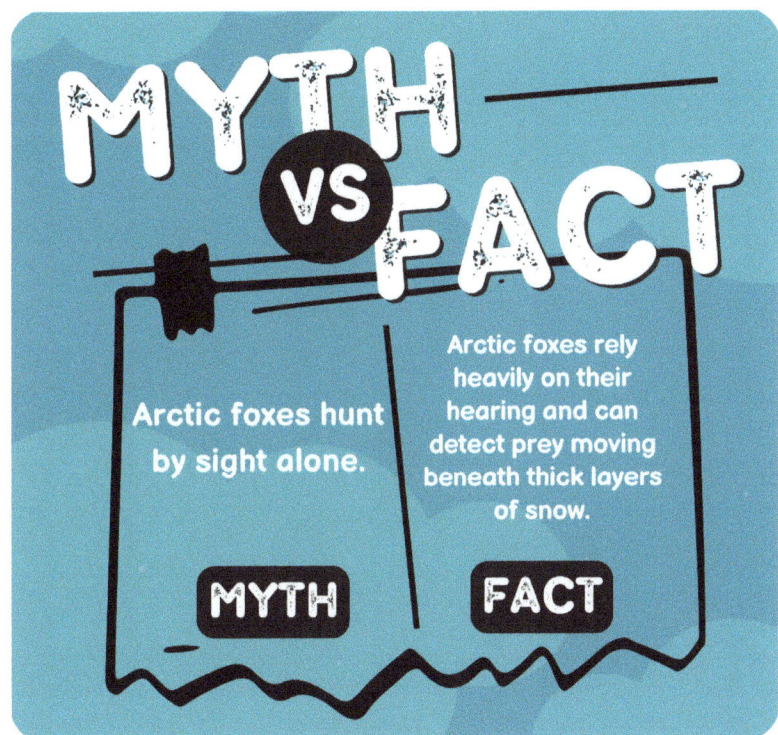

A Day in the Life

What does an ordinary day look like for an Arctic fox? It depends entirely on the season and on the dramatic cycle of light and darkness in the far north.

Summer Days
During the Arctic summer, the sun never sets. Daylight lasts 24 hours a day. Arctic foxes take advantage of this constant light to hunt whenever they are hungry. They are most active during the cooler hours and often rest during the warmest part of the day.

A typical summer day involves nonstop hunting. With pups to feed, parents work constantly to catch lemmings, raid bird nests, and gather food. Between hunts, they play with their growing pups near the den entrance, teaching them how to pounce and chase. Summer is a time of plenty, and smart foxes cache extra food for the long winter ahead.

Winter Days

Winter brings the opposite extreme. Weeks of near-total darkness settle over the Arctic as the sun barely rises above the horizon. Temperatures plunge, and Arctic foxes become more active during the darker hours, even though the difference between night and day nearly disappears.

Winter days are focused on survival. Foxes spend hours hunting beneath the snow, following polar bears across sea ice, or digging up food they stored months earlier. Between hunts, they curl into tight balls to conserve energy, wrapping their thick tails around their faces like furry scarves. They may sleep for long stretches and slow their metabolism to save precious calories.

Even during fierce blizzards, Arctic foxes often sleep right on top of the snow. Their incredible coats keep them warm without the need to retreat underground.

Life in the Den

A Fox Family Home
Home for an Arctic fox is an underground den, and these are far more than simple holes in the ground. Arctic fox dens are elaborate tunnel systems that also serve as social centers for fox families.

A good den site is precious in the frozen Arctic. Foxes dig their dens into hillsides, cliff bases, or raised mounds where the soil drains well and will not flood. Over many generations, fox families expand these burrows into massive underground mazes.

Life in a Skulk
Arctic foxes usually live in family groups called skulks. A typical skulk includes a breeding pair and their kits, and sometimes older daughters from previous years that help care for the young. Family members cooperate closely, sharing food and protecting the den from intruders.

Ancient Tunnel Systems
Some Arctic fox dens are centuries old and have been used by countless generations. Scientists have found dens with more than 100 entrances spread across an area the size of a tennis court. The tunnels can reach about 10 feet (3 meters) underground and stretch for hundreds of feet in total length. Multiple entrances give foxes many escape routes if predators approach.

Communication and Cooperation
Communication is key to life in a skulk. Arctic foxes use scent marking, body posture, and a wide range of sounds to communicate. They bark, yelp, whine, and scream to warn of danger, defend territory, and keep track of family members across the tundra.

A Shelter From the Storm
Inside the den, special chambers serve as nurseries where mothers give birth and raise their kits. Underground temperatures stay relatively stable compared to the brutal cold above, providing a safe refuge from Arctic storms.

During blizzards, Arctic foxes may also dig temporary snow dens. They tunnel into a snowbank, curl up with their fluffy tail wrapped around their face, and wait out the worst weather in their icy shelter.

Mating and Birth

Arctic foxes are monogamous and usually mate for life, staying with the same partner year after year. If one mate dies, the survivor may find a new partner, but many pairs remain together for their entire lives.

Finding a Mate

Breeding season begins in early spring, from February through April, when the long Arctic winter slowly starts to fade. Males and females that do not already have partners search for one another using scent markings and vocal calls. Arctic foxes make a surprising range of sounds, including barks, screams, and high-pitched howls that echo across the frozen tundra.

The Pregnancy

After mating, females are pregnant for about 52 days, which is less than two months. As the birth approaches, the mother prepares the den by cleaning out old chambers and creating a warm nursery lined with fur and feathers.

Birth and Babies

Arctic fox babies are called kits, or pups. Litters usually include 5 to 10 kits, but when food is plentiful, a mother may give birth to as many as 14 babies. This is one of the largest litter sizes of any wild member of the dog family.

> **NEWBORN KIT STATS**
> - Birth weight: about 2 oz (57 g)
> - Eyes open: 10–14 days
> - First steps: 2–3 week
> - Leaving the den: 3–4 weeks
> - Weaning: 6–10 weeks

Newborn kits are tiny, blind, deaf, and completely helpless. They are covered in short, dark fur and weigh only about 2 ounces (57 grams), roughly the weight of a chicken egg. For the first few weeks of life, they depend entirely on their mother's milk and warmth.

Both parents help raise the young. While the mother stays in the den nursing the kits, the father hunts constantly, bringing back lemmings, birds, and other food to support his growing family.

Growing Up Arctic Fox

Life as an Arctic fox kit is a race against time. Babies must grow quickly before the brutal winter arrives.

First Weeks
Newborn kits spend their first weeks in the dark safety of the den, snuggled together for warmth and nursing often. Their eyes open at about two weeks, revealing the curious gaze they will need as hunters. By three weeks, they can hear, and their tiny teeth begin to appear.

Venturing Out
Around four weeks old, kits take their first wobbly steps outside the den. The outside world is full of new sights and smells, and in summer the sun may shine all day and night. At first, kits stay close to the den entrance, tumbling over one another and pouncing on imaginary prey.

Learning to Hunt
As kits grow, playtime turns into practice. They chase each other, stalk insects, and pounce on anything that moves, including blowing grass and their siblings' tails. These games build strength, coordination, and hunting instincts.

By six weeks, kits begin eating solid food brought back by their parents. By about ten weeks, they start catching insects and small prey on their own. Parents teach by example as kits follow along on short hunting trips.

DID YOU KNOW?
Arctic fox families are sometimes surprisingly large! In addition to the parents and their kits, some dens include "helper" foxes—usually older daughters from the previous year who stick around to help raise their younger siblings.

Growing Up
Arctic fox kits grow incredibly fast and reach nearly adult size by fall, just in time for their first winter. As autumn arrives, the family group begins to break apart. Young foxes leave to find their own territories, sometimes traveling many miles. Some females stay near their mother and may help raise the next year's litter.

Fun Fact: Arctic fox kits learn to hunt by playing with their siblings.

Fun Fact: Scientists can spot ancient Arctic fox dens from space because the vegetation around them is greener than the surrounding tundra.

Arctic Foxes and Their Ecosystem

Arctic foxes play a vital role in the frozen ecosystems where they live. They are both predator and prey, making them an important link in the Arctic food web.

Population Controllers

As predators, Arctic foxes help keep lemming and vole populations in check. Without foxes hunting them, these rodents could multiply quickly and over-graze tundra vegetation. By eating rodents, foxes help maintain the delicate balance of Arctic life.

Food for Others

Arctic foxes are not at the top of the food chain. They serve as prey for larger predators such as wolves, wolverines, golden eagles, and polar bears. Healthy fox populations help support these hunters and strengthen the entire Arctic predator community.

Ecosystem Engineers

Arctic fox dens do more than shelter fox families. Over time, the soil around these dens becomes enriched by droppings, leftover food, and decomposing prey. This creates patches of thicker, greener vegetation in the otherwise sparse tundra. These areas provide food and shelter for insects, birds, and small mammals.

DID YOU KNOW?

By hunting rodents and scavenging leftovers, Arctic foxes help keep Arctic ecosystems balanced and healthy.

Scavengers and Cleaners

By following polar bears and feeding on leftover kills, Arctic foxes help recycle nutrients back into the ecosystem. They also eat carrion, or dead animals, which helps reduce the spread of disease. In this way, Arctic foxes act as the Arctic's cleanup crew.

Seed Spreaders

When Arctic foxes eat berries and other plants, they spread seeds across the tundra in their droppings. This helps plants grow in new areas and supports healthy, diverse tundra vegetation.

Natural Predators

Despite being skilled hunters themselves, Arctic foxes face danger from several larger predators in their frozen world.

Wolves

Gray wolves and Arctic wolves are among the most dangerous threats to Arctic foxes. A fox caught in the open has little chance against these powerful hunters. Wolves may kill Arctic foxes for food or to eliminate competition, since foxes hunt some of the same prey.

Red Foxes

Perhaps the Arctic fox's biggest rival is its close cousin, the red fox. Red foxes are larger and more aggressive, and where their territories overlap, they usually dominate. Red foxes may kill Arctic foxes and take over their dens. As the Arctic warms, red foxes are moving farther north, increasing pressure on Arctic fox populations.

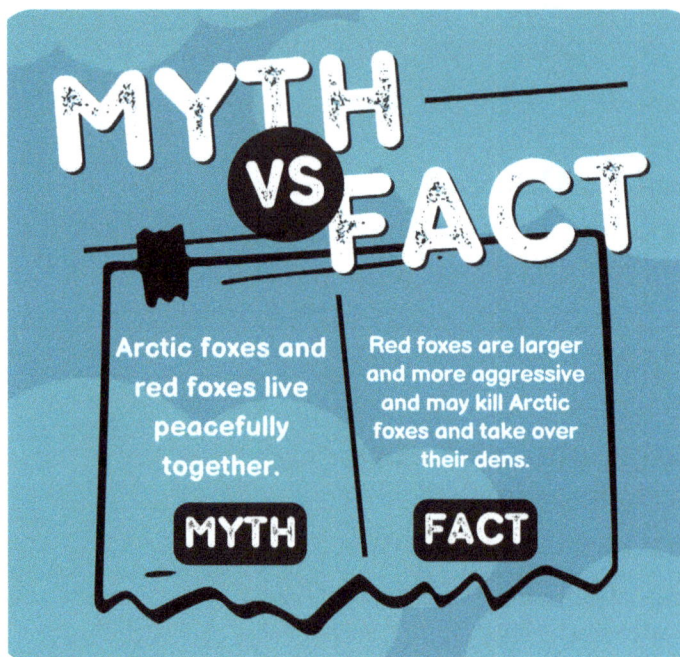

MYTH VS FACT

Arctic foxes and red foxes live peacefully together. **MYTH**

Red foxes are larger and more aggressive and may kill Arctic foxes and take over their dens. **FACT**

Polar Bears

Arctic foxes often follow polar bears in hopes of scavenging leftovers, but the relationship can be dangerous. Polar bears will eat Arctic foxes if given the chance, so foxes must keep their distance to avoid becoming prey themselves.

Birds of Prey

Golden eagles, snowy owls, and other large birds of prey hunt Arctic foxes from above. Kits and young foxes are especially vulnerable to attacks from the air.

Wolverines

Wolverines are fierce predators that will attack almost anything, including Arctic foxes. They sometimes raid fox dens to kill and eat the kits inside.

Arctic foxes survive by staying alert, using their speed and agility to escape danger, and retreating to their dens when threatened. Multiple den entrances provide critical escape routes when predators approach.

Fun Fact: Arctic fox dens often have many entrances so foxes can escape predators quickly.

Fun Fact: In parts of Scandinavia, conservationists provide extra food during winter to help Arctic fox populations recover.

Challenges and Threats

Beyond natural predators, Arctic foxes face growing challenges in a rapidly changing world, many of them caused by humans.

Climate Change
The greatest threat to Arctic foxes is climate change. The Arctic is warming faster than any other region on Earth, creating serious problems for these cold-adapted animals.

As temperatures rise, red foxes are moving farther north into Arctic fox territory. Red foxes are larger and more aggressive and often outcompete Arctic foxes for food and den sites. In some areas, Arctic fox populations have declined sharply as red foxes take over.

Warming temperatures also affect sea ice, which coastal Arctic foxes depend on for food. Less ice means fewer opportunities to follow polar bears and scavenge seal remains. Winter rain can freeze into thick ice layers that trap lemmings beneath the snow, making them unreachable.

Habitat Loss
Roads, pipelines, mines, and other development are breaking up Arctic fox habitat. These barriers can separate foxes from hunting areas, dens, and potential mates.

Hunting and Trapping
For centuries, Arctic foxes were hunted for their fur. Although this has declined in many places due to legal protections and changing demand, trapping still occurs in some regions.

Disease
As new animals move north with warming temperatures, they bring diseases Arctic foxes have little resistance to. Illnesses such as rabies and mange can spread quickly and severely reduce populations.

What's Being Done
Conservation programs are working to protect Arctic foxes. Scientists track foxes using GPS collars to better understand their movements and needs. Some countries have established protected areas and emergency feeding programs. Long-term protection depends on slowing climate change and preserving Arctic habitats.

Life Span and Population

Arctic foxes live relatively short lives in the wild. Most survive 3 to 6 years in one of the harshest environments on Earth. A small number that avoid predators, disease, and starvation may live 10 years or longer. In captivity, where food is reliable and predators are absent, Arctic foxes can live up to 15 years.

The first year of life is the most dangerous. Only about half of all kits survive to their first birthday. Young foxes must learn to hunt, avoid predators, and survive their first Arctic winter while they are still growing. Those that make it through this critical year are well adapted to life in the frozen north.

DID YOU KNOW?

Arctic fox populations can change dramatically from year to year depending on lemming numbers.

Population Numbers

Worldwide, there are several hundred thousand Arctic foxes, though exact numbers are difficult to measure across their vast and remote range. Globally, the species is not considered endangered and is listed as Least Concern by the International Union for Conservation of Nature.

However, this overall stability hides serious regional problems. In Scandinavia, Arctic fox populations dropped to fewer than 200 individuals and remain critically endangered despite ongoing protection efforts. Small, isolated populations in parts of Russia and other regions face similar risks.

The Lemming Connection

Arctic fox populations rise and fall with lemming numbers in a natural cycle that repeats every 3 to 4 years. When lemmings are abundant, foxes have large litters and populations increase. When lemming numbers crash, many foxes starve and populations decline. This cycle has existed for thousands of years, but climate change is making lemming populations less predictable.

Conclusion

Arctic foxes are remarkable survivors. Small, fluffy, and incredibly tough, they are perfectly suited for one of the harshest environments on Earth.

In a world of endless winter, howling blizzards, and temperatures cold enough to freeze exposed skin in seconds, Arctic foxes do more than survive. They thrive. Their color-changing coats, heat-trapping fur, and furry feet are masterpieces of natural design. Their sharp hearing allows them to catch prey hidden beneath the snow. Their flexible diets and clever food-caching habits help them endure the leanest months.

But Arctic foxes are more than a collection of impressive adaptations. They are devoted parents that often mate for life and work together to raise their young. They are essential members of the Arctic ecosystem, helping control rodent populations, feeding larger predators, and shaping the landscape through their ancient dens. They are survivors that have endured ice ages and thrived in conditions that challenge even the best-equipped human explorers.

Today, Arctic foxes face new challenges. Climate change is warming their frozen world, bringing new competitors and disrupting the balance they depend on. Yet Arctic foxes have adapted to extreme conditions for thousands of years. With continued efforts to protect Arctic habitats and slow climate change, these resilient animals can continue to roam the tundra far into the future.

The next time you shiver on a cold winter day, think of the Arctic fox curled up on open snow with its tail wrapped around its nose, calm and comfortable in temperatures that would stop most animals in their tracks. That is one tough little fox.

Test Your Arctic Fox Knowledge!

Think you remember everything about these amazing Arctic survivors? See how many questions you can answer!

❄ 1. What does the Arctic fox's scientific name, *Vulpes lagopus*, mean?
A) Snow fox B) White wolf C) Hare-footed fox D) Ice hunter

❄ 2. True or False: Arctic foxes have the warmest fur of any mammal on Earth.

❄ 3. What is the Arctic fox's favorite food?
A) Fish B) Lemmings C) Berries D) Seaweed

❄ 4. How cold can it get before an Arctic fox starts to shiver?
A) 32°F (0°C) B) 0°F (-18°C) C) -40°F (-40°C) D) -94°F (-70°C)

❄ 5. What color do most Arctic foxes turn in summer?
A) White B) Brown or gray C) Black D) Red

❄ 6. What are baby Arctic foxes called?
A) Pups B) Cubs C) Kits D) Both A and C

❄ 7. Which animal is moving into Arctic fox territory due to climate change?
A) Polar bears B) Red foxes C) Wolves D) Snowy owls

❄ 8. How do Arctic foxes hunt prey hidden under the snow?
A) They dig random holes B) They use their incredible hearing C) They wait for prey to come out D) They use their sense of smell only

❄ 9. Why do Arctic foxes follow polar bears?
A) For protection from wolves
B) To scavenge leftover seal meat
C) To steal their dens
D) To stay warm

❄ 10. How long can some Arctic fox dens be used?
A) 1-2 years B) 10-20 years C) 50-100 years D) Over 300 years

Answer Key: 1-C, 2-True, 3-B, 4-D, 5-B, 6-D, 7-B, 8-B, 9-B, 10-D

STEM Challenge: Think Like a Scientist!

Arctic foxes survive some of the coldest conditions on Earth. Try these fun, hands-on science experiments to discover how their amazing adaptations help them thrive in the frozen Arctic!

Arctic Insulation Test

Topic: Adaptation & Heat Transfer

You'll Need:
2 small jars or cups, 2 thermometers, cotton balls, rubber bands, warm water, timer

What to Do:
1. Fill both jars with the same amount of warm water and record the starting temperature.
2. Wrap one jar thickly with cotton balls and secure with rubber bands (this is your "arctic fox fur").
3. Leave the other jar unwrapped.
4. Place both jars in the refrigerator or outside on a cold day.
5. Check the temperature every 10 minutes for one hour.

What You'll Learn:
The insulated jar stays warmer longer—just like an Arctic fox's thick fur traps body heat! Their hollow hairs create air pockets that work even better than cotton.Snowshoe Science

Color-Changing Camouflage

Topic: Animal Adaptation & Survival

You'll Need:
White paper, brown paper, scissors, a friend, timer, grassy area and snowy area (or white and brown blankets)

What to Do:
1. Cut 10 small fox shapes from white paper and 10 from brown paper.
2. Have a friend scatter all 20 foxes on snow or a white blanket while you look away.
3. Set a timer for 30 seconds and collect as many as you can find.
4. Repeat on grass or a brown blanket.
5. Count which colors were easiest to find in each environment.

What You'll Learn:
White foxes are nearly invisible on snow but easy to spot on brown ground—and vice versa! This is why arctic foxes change color with the seasons.

Word Search

```
E W F M S K L U K S V Q A S M
J S V S P E C I E S N T L E P
C T O K O A D A P T A T I O N
S A M N O I T A V R E S N O C
T T N D B W H W D N W W I T Y
I I I U T N E P O N D L D E G
K B V I T Q X I T O E M R G Y
Y A O I C N T O E C N P E W Z
M H R X X A Q T I T D R G Z F
V O E X R G A S S U W O A H M
M C N E W N S W H R X T L K K
F A N O R H O K Y N D A F H A
L E M E G R U L Q A D D U K R
G P B M R A R N W L N E O Z C
O I P U A X M R T X K R M E T
H Y B W R L Y O K I P P A F I
N O M A D S S D U T N O C Y C
V N A P S E F I L S N G O B K
```

ADAPTATION	HIBERNATE	NOMADS
ARCTIC	HUNTING	OMNIVORE
BURROWS	KITS	PELT
CAMOUFLAGE	LIFESPAN	PREDATOR
CONSERVATION	MAMMALS	PREY
GENERATION	MONOGAMOUS	SKULK
HABITAT	NOCTURNAL	SPECIES

Glossary

adaptations – special features or behaviors that help a plant or animal survive in its environment

Arctic – the northernmost region of Earth, around the North Pole, where it's extremely cold and much of the ground stays frozen year-round

cache – to hide or store food for later use; arctic foxes bury extra food in the frozen ground

camouflage – coloring or patterns that help an animal blend in with its surroundings to hide from predators or prey

Canidae – the scientific family that includes dogs, wolves, and foxes

climate change – long-term changes in expected weather patterns, including rising temperatures

conservation – protecting natural resources, habitats, and wildlife for future generations

den – an underground shelter where animals live and raise their young

ecosystem – all the living things and their environment in a particular area, and how they interact

endangered species – a species that is in danger of becoming extinct

generation – offspring born at the same time; or the average time between a parent's birth and their offspring's birth

habitat – the natural home or environment where a plant or animal lives

hibernate – to enter a dormant or deep sleep state to conserve energy during winter

kits – baby foxes (also called pups)

mammals – warm-blooded animals with hair or fur that give birth to live young and feed them milk

monogamous – having only one mate; a bonded pair that stays together

nocturnal – most active at night

nomads – animals that move from place to place rather than staying in one territory

omnivore – an animal that eats both plants and meat

predator – an animal that hunts other animals for food

prey – an animal that is hunted by another animal for food

scavenger – an animal that feeds on dead animals it did not kill

skulk – a group of foxes

tundra – flat, treeless Arctic land where the ground stays permanently frozen beneath the surface

Resources and References

Want to learn more about Arctic foxes and the frozen north? Check out these trusted books, websites, and organizations that explore wildlife, science, and conservation in the Arctic.

Books

Arctic Foxes by Ruth Owen (Bearport Publishing) — Stunning photos and fascinating facts about these incredible survivors.

Animals of the Arctic by Peggy Thomas (Capstone Press) — Discover how Arctic species adapt to life in extreme cold.

The Arctic Habitat by Molly Aloian (Crabtree Publishing) — Explore the frozen world where arctic foxes make their home.

Life in the Tundra by Laura Purdie Salas (Capstone Press) — Learn about the plants and animals of this unique ecosystem.

Websites

National Geographic Kids – Arctic Fox
kids.nationalgeographic.com/animals/mammals/facts/arctic-fox
Amazing photos, videos, and facts about arctic fox adaptations and behavior.

World Wildlife Fund (WWF) – Arctic Fox
worldwildlife.org/species/arctic-fox
Learn about conservation efforts protecting arctic foxes and their habitat.

San Diego Zoo Wildlife Alliance – Arctic Fox
animals.sandiegozoo.org/animals/arctic-fox
Detailed information about arctic fox biology, diet, and family life.

Arctic Portal
arcticportal.org
Maps, news, and scientific updates about Arctic climate and ecosystems.

For Young Scientists

NASA Climate Kids
climatekids.nasa.gov
Understand how climate change affects the Arctic and animals like the arctic fox.

NOAA Arctic Program
arctic.noaa.gov
Scientific research and data about the changing Arctic environment.

Keep Exploring!

If you enjoyed learning about arctic foxes, explore other titles in the *This Incredible Planet* series to discover more amazing animals—from lions to reindeer to puffins—and the habitats they call home.

Index